MW01173572

The Only

Shadow Work

Journal You'll

Ever Need

HOW TO TAP INTO YOUR SUBCONSCIOUS
AND WORK THROUGH SPECIFIC BLOCKS
USING THE TAROT

The Psychic Shadow Worker

BEC RUDOLPH

The Only Shadow Work Journal You'll Ever Need: How to Tap Into Your Subconscious and Work Through Specific Blocks Using the Tarot

Published by TURQUOISE MOON PRESS
Westfield, Indiana, U.S.A.

Copyright ©2022 BEC RUDOLPH. All rights reserved.

No part of this book may be reproduced in any form or by any mechanical means, including information storage and retrieval systems without permission in writing from the publisher/author, except by a reviewer who may quote passages in a review.

All images, logos, quotes, and trademarks included in this book are subject to use according to trademark and copyright laws of the United States of America.

RUDOLPH, BEC, Author
THE ONLY SHADOW WORK JOURNAL YOU'LL EVER NEED
BEC RUDOLPH

ISBN: 979-8-9858496-0-8

BODY, MIND & SPIRIT / Divination / Tarot
SELF-HELP / Journaling

QUANTITY PURCHASES: Schools, companies, professional groups, clubs,

and other organizations may qualify for special terms when ordering quantities of this title. For information, email thepsychicshadowworker@gmail.com.

All rights reserved by BEC RUDOLPH and TURQUOISE MOON PRESS.

This book is printed in the United States of America.

TURQUOISE
MOON
PRESS

Part 1

Hello, amazing Shadow Worker!

I want to first congratulate you on your decision to start your Shadow Work journey! It is not an easy task, but I know you will find so much value and healing in making the decision to face your Shadow.

Before we get started, I want to talk about what your Shadow is. Once upon a time, you experienced a trauma or challenge. (Either a onetime event or a repeating pattern.) It was something that might have been outside of your capacity to handle properly at the time. Your Shadow is the result of that. Your inner being, subconscious, mind, soul, whatever you want to call it, created a protection or a Shadow to help you cope.

Perhaps you experienced abandonment from people you were close to as a child. As an adult, your Shadow says, "Based off of my previous experiences, the likelihood of a person hurting us is high, so when I see you getting close to someone, I'm going to sabotage the relationship, so you don't get hurt like you did in your childhood."

Shadow-sabotage manifests as angry outbursts, emotional manipulation, closing yourself off, etc.

The problem is, chances are, you are no longer in the environment you were in that created the Shadow in the first place. The Shadow is no longer serving you, but it thinks it is. Yours shows up all the time, even when you don't realize it.

The first step in facing your Shadow is thanking it. That's right. Thank your Shadow for its protection. For helping you in the moments where you needed it.

And then *let it go*. This is where Shadow Work comes in. To let something go, we first must identify what it is we must let go of. We must work through it and reprogram our subconscious to serve us in the here and now.

Let your Shadow know it's okay to let go. That you are so grateful for it, but it is no longer needed. Imagine yourself giving it a hug and wrapping it in love and grace. And then imagine it floating away.

You can start your Shadow Work journey by writing a letter to your Shadow. Let it know all the thoughts that come up. How it helps you, how it hurts you, how you feel. Do not hold back. Remember; You. Are. Loved. Always. By your Shadow, by your soul, by me, your spirit guides, by God, by the Universe.

Your Shadow Work journal is a safe space. A place where you can write down everything and still be loved. No one has to see it. This journal is for you, the user, to bare your soul to cultivate radical transformation and radical healing. In this journal, you are safe.

Tarot Decks

I have designed this system for the newest person to Shadow Work, which is why it was important to me that I publish a beginners-Tarot deck to go with it. You are certainly not bound to The Psychic Shadow Worker Deck; you can use whatever deck you feel most connected to!

If you are new to Tarot though, and have a hard time interpreting traditional decks, The Psychic Shadow Worker deck may be a great option for you. I designed this deck to follow the traditional Tarot but simplified it down to what I call "buzzwords." When you pull a card, you can immediately see the words and traits associated with this card.

I highly encourage you to continue your journey of learning to read and interpret the traditional Tarot, but I did not want a struggle to read the cards to be a deterrent for anybody who wants to dive into Shadow Work. Thus, The Psychic Shadow Worker Deck was born. This deck is perfect for anyone starting at square one, or even for those who can appreciate a level of simplicity and minimalism. I know it will guide you into the ultimate path of healing and self-love.

Jumping In

One of the biggest questions I get asked as a Shadow Worker is "Where do I start?" Or "How do I start?" Followed up by "What do I even do?"

These questions inspired me to share the system I used to facilitate radical transformation in myself.

Many Shadow Work journals exist, and you can purchase them from just about anywhere. At the beginning of my Shadow Work journey though, I realized something about all of them; they had good prompts, great prompts even, but I struggled to connect with them fully. "Name your biggest childhood fear" might be thought inducing and insightful, but it wasn't getting down to the root of problems I was experiencing in that exact moment. Just like the moon's phases, the blocks that were relevant in my life at that moment were changing.

So how does one tap into that? How does someone find their individual blocks?

That is where the Tarot comes in! The Tarot is so many things, but my favorite is it's a channel that connects us to our subconscious. It is why so many times in a reading someone might say, "Yep, I knew that!" Or "I had a feeling." The Tarot is simply a way for us to reach into the innermost parts of ourselves. Some call it a Shadow, some a subconscious, others say Spirit, but at the end of the day no matter what you call it, it is YOU.

We can absolutely use this to our advantage... That's why it's there!

Why Shadow Work? What is so special about Shadow Work?

Let's break it down a little bit.

Let us say you are a hot air balloon, and every mental and spiritual block you have is a bag of sand tied to that balloon.

Now let us say all the best things in life (manifestation, love, Law of Attraction, self-love, acceptance, etc.) are operating at a vibrational level of 10. But the bags of sand/blocks are holding you down at a level of 5. By identifying these blocks and removing them, our hot air balloon can rise to higher frequencies and vibration levels.

7

Most of us spend our time looking up to level 10, wondering why we're not there. Yet, we do not remove the bags of sand holding us down because looking at our bags of sand might be too hard. We may not want to admit certain bags of sand are there or we may even be emotionally attached to some of them, fearing what would happen if we cut them loose.

By facing these blocks and making an intentional and conscious decision to remove them, we effectively raise our vibration!

Shadow Work is an incredible tool in doing just that, raising our vibration to become synchronized with our Highest Self.

You cannot manifest money if you subconsciously believe you are not worthy of money. If you did, you might spend it all away immediately because your comfort zone is that of not having it- remember what we talked about with sabotage? You cannot manifest a soulmate if you are not in a vibration to attract one. You cannot become a best-selling author if you believe in your heart that you are not a good writer.

All the best things in life are right on the other side of what you are afraid to face. Right on the other side of fear.

Shadow Work is the tool for identifying these fears, facing them, working through them, and finally, replacing them with beliefs that serve us.

Disclaimer

Shadow Work can be a triggering process. It is important to stay aware of your body and mental state as you start and continue this journey. Use discretion and honor yourself and listen to your body. Shadow Work is not meant to replace traditional therapy and I advocate for doing Shadow Work in conjunction with therapy. They are both valuable for their own reasons and can never be a replacement for the other.

How to Use this Journal

The idea behind this journal is simplicity. The simpler something is, the more likely we will take the time to do it. This journal has enough pages for 8 weeks of Shadow Sessions. There is one Diagnostic section and four Check-In Sections per week. An example of what your week could look like is:

Monday: Diagnostic Spread

Tuesday: Check-In Spread

Wednesday: Check-In Spread

Thursday: Check-In Spread

Friday: Check-In Spread

Saturday: Rest! Take time to do something creative, go for a walk, or read!

Sunday: Rest! Plan out your upcoming week or practice your Tarot skills!

You don't have to use this journal for the full five allotted days per week, but the more consistent you are, the more likely you will create the habit of sitting down and prioritizing time for you.

Check-In and Spiritual Hygiene

Before each session, I have provided an area for you to "check-in." That way you can clear your mind easier. This space is for you to assess how you feel emotionally in that moment before you dive deeper. Move down the Spiritual Hygiene checklist and cross off each item as you go. (I explain how to do the *energetic* portion of this routine later.) It's not required to do breathwork or stretch, but it's not a bad idea! Breath or bodywork can be incorporated at any point of the check-in. They can also enhance the benefits of every item on this list, so you might as well!

Diagnostics Section

Use this section for when you have the time and energy to sit down for a 15–30-minute Shadow Work session. Ask the Tarot to show you blocks you should be working through in the immediate future and follow the prompts for how to smash and replace them.

For the sake of simplicity, I only provide four spots for cards in the Diagnostic Spread. While it can be tempting to do much larger spreads in our Shadow Work journey, (and sometimes necessary) the goal is to chip away a little at a time. Consistency is where the real growth happens. By only doing four cards, we are homing in on specific energy.

In a Diagnostic Spread you should ask the Tarot, "What blocks should I be focusing on today?" "What energy can I improve on?"

Let's say you pulled the Sun (which I tend to see associated with the inner child) and the Five of Cups. We know the Cups represent relationships and basic numerology tells us that five is a number representing conflict or strife. Perhaps you felt lonely as a child or were isolated often and did not have many meaningful relationships. You have a limiting belief or block that you are not someone others want to be around in the present day.

So how do we use this knowledge of blockages to remove them? That brings us to the next portion of the Diagnostics section, *Reflection*.

Reflection

Use the Reflection portion of the Diagnostic pages to brain dump. How does this make you feel? When do you think this blockage began? Who gave you this limiting belief? How does it affect you today? Reflect on the ways the blocks have affected your life.

The *Questions to Ponder* section is to write down any further questions you might have, need more time to think about, or things you want to return to in a later Shadow Work session. This section is optional.

The next step, however, is vital; write down *Actionable Steps* you can take to remove your block/s.

Maybe you don't feel free to express your personal style. An actionable step to removing this block might be to wear something today that you have always wanted to but were previously afraid to.

Maybe a block is that you never stand up for yourself, so you write that the next time someone cuts you down verbally, you will verbally set the boundary that they can no longer do that, or perhaps walk away entirely.

These steps do not necessarily have to happen the day you write them, but they should always be considered when the block comes up.

Gratitude

Next, you will write down three things you are grateful for today. A mindset of gratitude can change your life. You will start seeing your life from an abundance mindset which will manifest more abundance! It is one of the most effective things you can do when committing to raising your vibration. Challenge yourself and write three new things every time you sit down for a Shadow Work session. See how many days you can go with no repeats!

Affirmations

Lastly, you will write your affirmations. These can be anything you feel now. You can also use the "opposite rule." This just means whatever your blockage is, you will affirm the opposite. For example:

Block: I do not have enough skills to pursue my dream job

Affirmation: I am skillful. I am capable of acquiring new skills and I am a quick learner.

Block: I am not worthy of love

Affirmation: I am love. I am loved.

Avoid saying "I will" statements and instead use "I am." "Will" implies it happens in the future and there is no concrete future, but there is concrete now. Affirm it in the now and you are bound to see it in the future!

Challenge yourself by saying these things aloud. I know it may feel silly, but the more comfortable you get with affirming these new beliefs, the better!

Check-Up Section

This section is for those days when you may only have 5-10 minutes to spare for connecting with your Tarot and Shadow, or in the days following a heavier Diagnostic session. Ask the Tarot the questions provided or one you have come up with yourself and then follow the prompts for the rest of this section.

I know the title of this journal seems bold, but I truly feel like it is accurate. By tapping into your own subconscious and learning how to marry the Tarot and the art of removing those blockages and replacing them with new beliefs, you will never need another Shadow Work journal with random prompts again!

This is all about taking control of your transformation journey, and fast tracking it. It's about removing the most prevalent blocks in your life NOW. You don't have to wait years and years for the right prompt to find you. YOU decided to go out and find it. This is taking radical responsibility for your radical transformation!

Diving Deeper

I believe the way to get the most out of a Shadow Session is in the four pillars of a sacred space.

A sacred space is just that; a space you come to each day to do your most sacred work. Even if you do not have a lot of space, or you have little ones that like to touch everything, you can keep all your sacred space items in a box or drawer, ready to be pulled out for your Shadow Work session.

You want to set up your sacred space with items and tools that help you WANT to be in that space and that make you look forward to doing your work.

What are the Four Pillars of A Sacred Space?

The four pillars include:

Loving Items

Joyful Items

Healing Items

Work Items

Loving Items

These are items that make you feel loved when looking at them. This can include pictures of family and friends, pets, deities, anything that harbors a deep connection with love!

Joyful Items

These are items that make you feel joy. This can include little trinkets or postcards, incense or candles, anything that sparks happiness!

Healing Items

These are items that help foster a safe and healing space for you to work in. This can include crystals and plants, or even essential oils.

Work Items

This notebook, a pen, and your Tarot Deck are all you truly need to get to work.

Once you have your sacred space set up, it is time to get your energy ready for some Shadow Work.

Spiritual Hygiene

Spiritual Hygiene is an incredibly useful tool that you can use to center your energy. It's important to become centered before doing Shadow Work because as we go deeper into our emotions and blockages; we want to be sure they are *ours* and only ours. Sometimes as you go throughout your day or when you first wake up in the morning, you're vulnerable to energies and the people all around you. A lot of us tend to absorb those energies without even thinking about it so it's important to cleanse your energy and your space before starting Shadow Work. I took a psychic activation course by psychic, Emily Dexter, and she gives a three-step method to a good Spiritual Hygiene Routine. I've changed it around a little to fit me, feel free to do the same for yourself!

Cleansing

It is important to cleanse your energy and your space often. Physically, burning incense and lighting sage is a wonderful way to reset the energy in a room. Ringing a bell (or even clanking a pot and wooden spoon together!) can also cleanse your space. Even playing music has cleansing abilities. The purpose is to bring the room to a positive and safe vibration. One that is cleared of all negativities and is fresh.

Cleansing your body can also be done in a multitude of ways. There is of course physically cleansing yourself in the shower or bath (this has great physical *and* mental benefits) but there are other ways too.

When thinking of energy, it is important to tell any energy that is not yours to leave. That's right. Simply tell it to leave. You can say "Any thoughts, feelings, emotions, or energies that are not my own must leave my body and my space right now." You do not even have to say it aloud. We are more powerful than we think. Just setting the intention of cleansing most of the time is enough!

Grounding

There are many methods of grounding and it's unique to each person on what they like or what works best for them. My favorite method is calling energy to your third eye and then imagine shooting that energy down to the Earth's core. Once it hits the core, imagine it bouncing up all the way back to you. Then you will bounce it right back down. On and on until you feel grounded. Other methods include standing outside barefoot or visualizing the energy between the Earth and the bottom of your feet meeting. You can even come up with your own way! Do what works for you.

Protecting

Lastly, you want to protect this energy that you have worked so hard for. My favorite method is imagining bright silver light coming out of my skin starting with my arms, then spreading throughout the body. I just visualize it getting brighter and brighter and expanding outwards. Creating a protective bubble is even more important if you have a job where you are constantly around people or are a parent who wants to make sure you do not absorb the chaotic energy of toddlers or teenagers!

Example:

I have created an example Diagnostic section that you can review before you get started to help you understand how a session can go for you! Come back to this example as many times as you need.

I hope this journal helps guide into radical transformation and you find total self-love and acceptance at through this journey!

Bonus: The beginner's system to marrying Tarot and Shadow Work

The best way to understand how to marry these two concepts together is the Handprint of Energy.

Imagine each suit of the Tarot is a different finger. (Excluding the thumb.)

Cups

Pentacles

Swords

Wands

We know that each of these suits represents a different element or a different concept.

Cups -water - Emotions/ Relationships

Pentacles - Earth - Finances, material possessions

Swords - air- intellect/mindset and communication

Wands - fire - passion (in all areas, i.e., relationships, career, or home life) and sexuality

Anything in these suits represents our day-to-day life

And for the thumb we will think of it as major themes or the Major Arcana. Take each of your fingers and touch them to your thumb. You see how the Major Arcana/thumb can interact with each of the fingers?

This is because those major life themes affect our everyday life.

Use this system when interpreting your spreads and card pulls for better clarity!

Part 2

Date: ___Today___

Check in:

Today, I feel pretty good. I'm a little tired because I woke up a few times last night, but I know today will still be a good day

---

Alignment Routine

Energy

Cleanse

Ground

Protect

Body

Movement

Breathwork

Stretch

Meditate

DIAGNOSTIC TAROT SPREAD

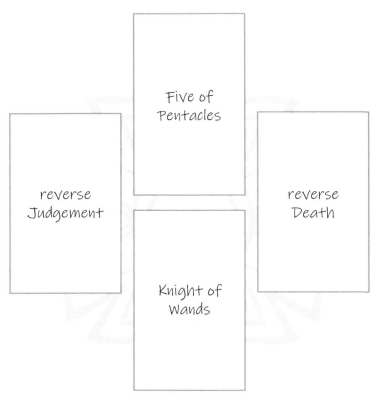

Five of
Pentacles

reverse
Judgement

reverse
Death

Knight of
Wands

 What block is the Tarot showing you?

Financial insecurity, hesitancy to move on, fear of letting go.

Reflection

The five of pentacles tells me there is a lack mindset. That I am feeling insecure about my finances so I am inclined to make some hasty and impulsive decisions. I think this is referencing my need to online shop. When I am feeling emotionally vulnerable or down in any way, I immediately go to add to cart and buy. This is probably why I pulled the Five of Pentacles. I have a lack mindset, I need material things to make me feel whole. The Judgment in reverse tells me I am hesitant to look inward, to understand why this is and the Death in reverse shows that I am hesitant to the transformation necessary to change this lack mindset. I think this stems from guilt. We didn't have a lot of money growing up, but my parents always did everything they could to provide for us.

Even though they did their best, I still remember how insecure I felt in those moments, in those times where we didn't have enough. I think by admitting my childhood financial problems and how they affected me then and now, it will make me a bad or unappreciative daughter. I know that by allowing

Reflection

myself to admit the insecurity I felt in those times, does not

make me a bad anything. Just acknowledging regular

human emotions that any child would feel in those moments.

When I was a kid, I thought if we just had more

money, and could afford more, that we would

be happier. Now that I am an adult, I know that

having more things won't make me happier.

Being secure, will. And the truth is I AM secure

Reflection

Reflection

Questions to ponder

What other things am I afraid to admit because

I don't want to hurt someone's feelings?

What other emotions have I blocked because I

feel guilty for feeling them?

 ACTIONABLE STEPS I CAN TAKE TO RELEASE/OVERCOME THIS BLOCK

The next time I feel the need to shop online,

I will do something that makes me feel

secure, like taking a warm bath or

go for a walk to ground myself.

THINGS I AM GRATEFUL FOR

1. My kids

2. Warm baths

3. My source of income that gives me security

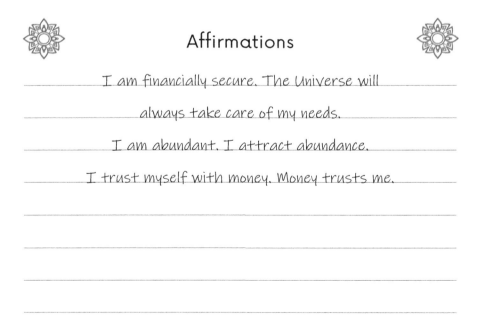

Affirmations

I am financially secure. The Universe will

always take care of my needs.

I am abundant. I attract abundance.

I trust myself with money. Money trusts me.

Week 1

Date: _____

Check in:

😊 🙂 😐 🙁

_____

_____

_____

_____

_____

Alignment Routine

Energy

Cleanse

Ground

Protect

Body

Movement

Breathwork

Stretch

Meditate

DIAGNOSTIC TAROT SPREAD

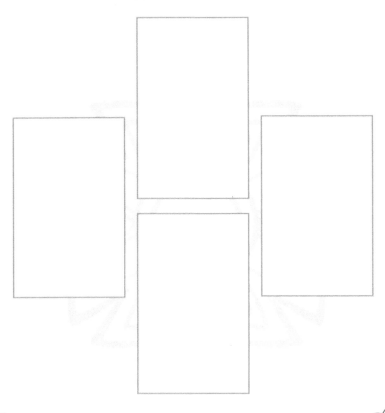

What block is the Tarot showing you?

_____

_____

_____

_____

_____

Reflection

_____

_____

_____

_____

_____

_____

_____

_____

_____

_____

_____

_____

_____

_____

_____

_____

_____

_____

_____

Reflection

Reflection

Questions to ponder

_____

_____

_____

_____

_____

_____

_____

_____

_____

 ## ACTIONABLE STEPS I CAN TAKE TO RELEASE/OVERCOME THIS BLOCK

THINGS I AM GRATEFUL FOR

1.

2.

3.

Affirmations

_____

_____

_____

_____

_____

_____

_____

_____

Date: _____

Check in:

😊 🙂 😐 ☹️

_____

_____

_____

_____

_____

Alignment Routine

Energy

Cleanse

Ground

Protect

Body

Movement

Breathwork

Stretch

Meditate

CHECK-UP

Ask the Tarot:
What energy should I
focus on or be aware of
today?

Ask the Tarot:
How can I embody
my highest good
today?

Reflection

Reflection

Questions to ponder

 ## ACTIONABLE STEPS I CAN TAKE TO RELEASE/OVERCOME THIS BLOCK

THINGS I AM GRATEFUL FOR

1.

2.

3.

Affirmations

Date: _____

Check in:

😊　🙂　😐　🙁

_____
_____
_____
_____
_____

Alignment Routine

Energy

Cleanse

Ground

Protect

Body

Movement

Breathwork

Stretch

Meditate

CHECK-UP

Ask the Tarot:
What energy should I
focus on or be aware of
today?

Ask the Tarot:
How can I embody
my highest good
today?

Reflection

Reflection

Questions to ponder

_____

_____

_____

_____

_____

_____

_____

_____

_____

_____

 ## ACTIONABLE STEPS I CAN TAKE TO RELEASE/OVERCOME THIS BLOCK

THINGS I AM GRATEFUL FOR

1.

2.

3.

Affirmations

_____

_____

_____

_____

_____

_____

_____

_____

Date: _____

Check in:

Alignment Routine

Energy

Cleanse

Ground

Protect

Body

Movement

Breathwork

Stretch

Meditate

CHECK-UP

Ask the Tarot:
What energy should I
focus on or be aware of
today?

Ask the Tarot:
How can I embody
my highest good
today?

Reflection

_____

_____

_____

_____

_____

_____

_____

_____

_____

_____

_____

_____

_____

_____

_____

_____

_____

_____

_____

_____

_____

Reflection

_____

_____

_____

_____

_____

_____

_____

_____

_____

_____

_____

_____

_____

_____

_____

_____

_____

_____

_____

_____

_____

Questions to ponder

_____

_____

_____

_____

_____

_____

_____

_____

_____

_____

 ACTIONABLE STEPS I CAN TAKE TO RELEASE/OVERCOME THIS BLOCK

THINGS I AM GRATEFUL FOR

1.

2.

3.

Affirmations

_____

_____

_____

_____

_____

_____

_____

_____

Date: _____

Check in:

😊 🙂 😐 🙁

_____
_____
_____
_____
_____

Alignment Routine

Energy

Cleanse

Ground

Protect

Body

Movement

Breathwork

Stretch

Meditate

CHECK-UP

Ask the Tarot:
What energy should I
focus on or be aware of
today?

Ask the Tarot:
How can I embody
my highest good
today?

Reflection

Reflection

_____

_____

_____

_____

_____

_____

_____

_____

_____

_____

_____

_____

_____

_____

_____

_____

_____

_____

Questions to ponder

_____

_____

_____

_____

_____

_____

_____

_____

_____

 ACTIONABLE STEPS I CAN TAKE TO
RELEASE/OVERCOME THIS BLOCK

THINGS I AM GRATEFUL FOR

1.

2.

3.

Affirmations

Date: _____

Check in:

😊 🙂 😐 🙁

_____
_____
_____
_____
_____

Alignment Routine

Energy

Cleanse

Ground

Protect

Body

Movement

Breathwork

Stretch

Meditate

CHECK-UP

Ask the Tarot:
What energy should I
focus on or be aware of
today?

Ask the Tarot:
How can I embody
my highest good
today?

Reflection

Reflection

_____
_____
_____
_____
_____
_____
_____
_____
_____
_____
_____
_____
_____
_____
_____
_____
_____
_____
_____
_____

Questions to ponder

_____

_____

_____

_____

_____

_____

_____

_____

_____

 ACTIONABLE STEPS I CAN TAKE TO
RELEASE/OVERCOME THIS BLOCK

THINGS I AM GRATEFUL FOR

1.

2.

3.

Affirmations

_____

_____

_____

_____

_____

_____

_____

_____

_____

Week 2

Date: _____

Check in:

😊 🙂 😐 🙁

_____

_____

_____

_____

_____

Alignment Routine

Energy

Cleanse

Ground

Protect

Body

Movement

Breathwork

Stretch

Meditate

DIAGNOSTIC TAROT SPREAD

What block is the Tarot showing you?

_____

_____

_____

_____

_____

Reflection

_____

_____

_____

_____

_____

_____

_____

_____

_____

_____

_____

_____

_____

_____

_____

_____

_____

_____

Reflection

Reflection

Questions to ponder

_____

_____

_____

_____

_____

_____

_____

_____

_____

 ACTIONABLE STEPS I CAN TAKE TO
RELEASE/OVERCOME THIS BLOCK

THINGS I AM GRATEFUL FOR

1.

2.

3.

Affirmations

_____

_____

_____

_____

_____

_____

_____

_____

_____

Date: _____

Check in:

😊 🙂 😐 🙁

_____
_____
_____
_____
_____

Alignment Routine

Energy

Cleanse

Ground

Protect

Body

Movement

Breathwork

Stretch

Meditate

CHECK-UP

Ask the Tarot:
What energy should I
focus on or be aware of
today?

Ask the Tarot:
How can I embody
my highest good
today?

Reflection

Reflection

Questions to ponder

_____

_____

_____

_____

_____

_____

_____

_____

 ACTIONABLE STEPS I CAN TAKE TO RELEASE/OVERCOME THIS BLOCK

THINGS I AM GRATEFUL FOR

1.

2.

3.

Affirmations

Date: _____

Check in:

😊   🙂   😐   🙁

_____

_____

_____

_____

_____

Alignment Routine

Energy

Cleanse

Ground

Protect

Body

Movement

Breathwork

Stretch

Meditate

CHECK-UP

Ask the Tarot:
What energy should I
focus on or be aware of
today?

Ask the Tarot:
How can I embody
my highest good
today?

Reflection

Reflection

Questions to ponder

_____

_____

_____

_____

_____

_____

_____

_____

_____

 ## ACTIONABLE STEPS I CAN TAKE TO RELEASE/OVERCOME THIS BLOCK

THINGS I AM GRATEFUL FOR

1.

2.

3.

Affirmations

Date: _____

Check in:

😊 🙂 😐 ☹️

_____

_____

_____

_____

_____

Alignment Routine

Energy

Cleanse

Ground

Protect

Body

Movement

Breathwork

Stretch

Meditate

CHECK-UP

Ask the Tarot:
What energy should I
focus on or be aware of
today?

Ask the Tarot:
How can I embody
my highest good
today?

Reflection

Reflection

Questions to ponder

 ACTIONABLE STEPS I CAN TAKE TO RELEASE/OVERCOME THIS BLOCK

THINGS I AM GRATEFUL FOR

1.

2.

3.

 Affirmations

_____

_____

_____

_____

_____

_____

_____

_____

_____

Date: _____

Check in:

😊 🙂 😐 🙁

_____
_____
_____
_____
_____

Alignment Routine

Energy

Cleanse

Ground

Protect

Body

Movement

Breathwork

Stretch

Meditate

CHECK-UP

Ask the Tarot:
What energy should I
focus on or be aware of
today?

Ask the Tarot:
How can I embody
my highest good
today?

Reflection

Reflection

_____

_____

_____

_____

_____

_____

_____

_____

_____

_____

_____

_____

_____

_____

_____

_____

_____

_____

_____

Questions to ponder

_____

_____

_____

_____

_____

_____

_____

_____

_____

 ## ACTIONABLE STEPS I CAN TAKE TO
RELEASE/OVERCOME THIS BLOCK

THINGS I AM GRATEFUL FOR

1.

2.

3.

Affirmations

_____

_____

_____

_____

_____

_____

_____

_____

_____

Date: _____

Check in:

_____
_____
_____
_____
_____

Alignment Routine

Energy

Cleanse

Ground

Protect

Body

Movement

Breathwork

Stretch

Meditate

CHECK-UP

Ask the Tarot:
What energy should I
focus on or be aware of
today?

Ask the Tarot:
How can I embody
my highest good
today?

Reflection

Reflection

Questions to ponder

_____

_____

_____

_____

_____

_____

_____

_____

_____

 ## ACTIONABLE STEPS I CAN TAKE TO
RELEASE/OVERCOME THIS BLOCK

THINGS I AM GRATEFUL FOR

1.

2.

3.

Affirmations

_____

_____

_____

_____

_____

_____

_____

_____

Week 3

Date: _____

Check in:

😊 🙂 😐 🙁

_____
_____
_____
_____
_____

Alignment Routine

Energy

Cleanse

Ground

Protect

Body

Movement

Breathwork

Stretch

Meditate

DIAGNOSTIC TAROT SPREAD

What block is the Tarot showing you?

Reflection

Reflection

Reflection

Questions to ponder

_____

_____

_____

_____

_____

_____

_____

_____

_____

_____

 ## ACTIONABLE STEPS I CAN TAKE TO RELEASE/OVERCOME THIS BLOCK

THINGS I AM GRATEFUL FOR

1.

2.

3.

Affirmations

_____

_____

_____

_____

_____

_____

_____

_____

Date: _____

Check in:

😊 🙂 😐 🙁

_____
_____
_____
_____
_____

Alignment Routine

Energy

Cleanse

Ground

Protect

Body

Movement

Breathwork

Stretch

Meditate

CHECK-UP

Ask the Tarot:
What energy should I
focus on or be aware of
today?

Ask the Tarot:
How can I embody
my highest good
today?

Reflection

Reflection

Questions to ponder

 ACTIONABLE STEPS I CAN TAKE TO RELEASE/OVERCOME THIS BLOCK

THINGS I AM GRATEFUL FOR

1.

2.

3.

 Affirmations

_____

_____

_____

_____

_____

_____

_____

_____

Date: _____

Check in:

😊 🙂 😐 🙁

_____
_____
_____
_____
_____

Alignment Routine

Energy

Cleanse

Ground

Protect

Body

Movement

Breathwork

Stretch

Meditate

CHECK-UP

Ask the Tarot:
What energy should I
focus on or be aware of
today?

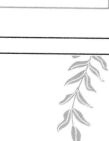

Ask the Tarot:
How can I embody
my highest good
today?

123

Reflection

Reflection

Questions to ponder

_____

_____

_____

_____

_____

_____

_____

_____

_____

 ACTIONABLE STEPS I CAN TAKE TO RELEASE/OVERCOME THIS BLOCK

THINGS I AM GRATEFUL FOR

1.

2.

3.

Affirmations

Date: _____

Check in:

😊　🙂　😐　🙁

_____

_____

_____

_____

_____

Alignment Routine

Energy

Cleanse

Ground

Protect

Body

Movement

Breathwork

Stretch

Meditate

CHECK-UP

Ask the Tarot:
What energy should I
focus on or be aware of
today?

Ask the Tarot:
How can I embody
my highest good
today?

Reflection

Reflection

Questions to ponder

_____

_____

_____

_____

_____

_____

_____

_____

 ACTIONABLE STEPS I CAN TAKE TO RELEASE/OVERCOME THIS BLOCK

THINGS I AM GRATEFUL FOR

1.

2.

3.

Affirmations

Date: _____

😊 🙂 😐 🙁

_____
_____
_____
_____
_____

Alignment Routine

Energy

Cleanse

Ground

Protect

Body

Movement

Breathwork

Stretch

Meditate

CHECK-UP

Ask the Tarot:
What energy should I
focus on or be aware of
today?

Ask the Tarot:
How can I embody
my highest good
today?

Reflection

Reflection

Questions to ponder

_____

_____

_____

_____

_____

_____

_____

_____

_____

 ## ACTIONABLE STEPS I CAN TAKE TO RELEASE/OVERCOME THIS BLOCK

THINGS I AM GRATEFUL FOR

1.

2.

3.

 Affirmations

_____

_____

_____

_____

_____

_____

_____

_____

Date: _____

Check in:

Alignment Routine

Energy

Cleanse

Ground

Protect

Body

Movement

Breathwork

Stretch

Meditate

CHECK-UP

Ask the Tarot:
What energy should I
focus on or be aware of
today?

Ask the Tarot:
How can I embody
my highest good
today?

Reflection

Reflection

Questions to ponder

_____

_____

_____

_____

_____

_____

_____

_____

_____

 ### ACTIONABLE STEPS I CAN TAKE TO
RELEASE/OVERCOME THIS BLOCK

THINGS I AM GRATEFUL FOR

1.

2.

3.

Affirmations

_____

_____

_____

_____

_____

_____

_____

_____

Week 4

Date: _____

Check in:

😊 🙂 😐 🙁

_____
_____
_____
_____
_____

Alignment Routine

Energy

Cleanse

Ground

Protect

Body

Movement

Breathwork

Stretch

Meditate

DIAGNOSTIC TAROT SPREAD

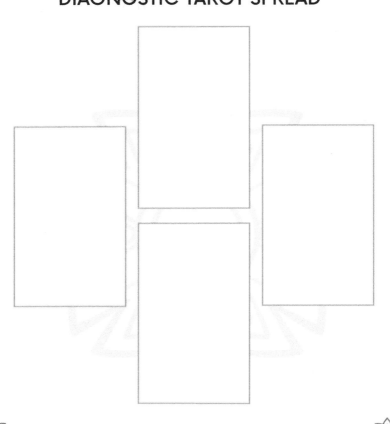

What block is the Tarot showing you?

_____

_____

_____

_____

_____

Reflection

Reflection

_____

_____

_____

_____

_____

_____

_____

_____

_____

_____

_____

_____

_____

_____

_____

_____

_____

Reflection

Questions to ponder

_____

_____

_____

_____

_____

_____

_____

_____

_____

_____

 ACTIONABLE STEPS I CAN TAKE TO RELEASE/OVERCOME THIS BLOCK

THINGS I AM GRATEFUL FOR

1.

2.

3.

Affirmations

Date: _____

Check in:

😊 🙂 😐 🙁

_____
_____
_____
_____
_____

Alignment Routine

Energy

Cleanse

Ground

Protect

Body

Movement

Breathwork

Stretch

Meditate

CHECK-UP

Ask the Tarot:
What energy should I
focus on or be aware of
today?

Ask the Tarot:
How can I embody
my highest good
today?

Reflection

Reflection

Questions to ponder

_____

_____

_____

_____

_____

_____

_____

_____

_____

 ## ACTIONABLE STEPS I CAN TAKE TO RELEASE/OVERCOME THIS BLOCK

THINGS I AM GRATEFUL FOR

1.

2.

3.

Affirmations

_____

_____

_____

_____

_____

_____

_____

_____

_____

Date: _____

Check in:

😊 🙂 😐 🙁

_____

_____

_____

_____

_____

Alignment Routine

Energy

Cleanse

Ground

Protect

Body

Movement

Breathwork

Stretch

Meditate

CHECK-UP

Ask the Tarot:
What energy should I
focus on or be aware of
today?

Ask the Tarot:
How can I embody
my highest good
today?

Reflection

Reflection

_____

_____

_____

_____

_____

_____

_____

_____

_____

_____

_____

_____

_____

_____

_____

_____

_____

_____

_____

Questions to ponder

_____

_____

_____

_____

_____

_____

_____

_____

_____

 **ACTIONABLE STEPS I CAN TAKE TO
RELEASE/OVERCOME THIS BLOCK**

THINGS I AM GRATEFUL FOR

1.

2.

3.

Affirmations

_____

_____

_____

_____

_____

_____

_____

_____

Date: _____

Check in:

😊 🙂 😐 🙁

_____
_____
_____
_____
_____

Alignment Routine

Energy

Cleanse

Ground

Protect

Body

Movement

Breathwork

Stretch

Meditate

CHECK-UP

Ask the Tarot:
What energy should I
focus on or be aware of
today?

Ask the Tarot:
How can I embody
my highest good
today?

Reflection

Reflection

_____

_____

_____

_____

_____

_____

_____

_____

_____

_____

_____

_____

_____

_____

_____

_____

_____

_____

_____

Questions to ponder

_____

_____

_____

_____

_____

_____

_____

_____

_____

 ACTIONABLE STEPS I CAN TAKE TO RELEASE/OVERCOME THIS BLOCK

THINGS I AM GRATEFUL FOR

1.

2.

3.

Affirmations

_____

_____

_____

_____

_____

_____

_____

_____

Date: _____

Check in:

😊 🙂 😐 ☹️

_____
_____
_____
_____
_____

Alignment Routine

Energy

Cleanse

Ground

Protect

Meditate

Body

Movement

Breathwork

Stretch

CHECK-UP

Ask the Tarot:
What energy should I
focus on or be aware of
today?

Ask the Tarot:
How can I embody
my highest good
today?

Reflection

Reflection

_____

_____

_____

_____

_____

_____

_____

_____

_____

_____

_____

_____

_____

_____

_____

_____

_____

_____

Questions to ponder

_____

_____

_____

_____

_____

_____

_____

_____

_____

 ACTIONABLE STEPS I CAN TAKE TO RELEASE/OVERCOME THIS BLOCK

THINGS I AM GRATEFUL FOR

1.

2.

3.

Affirmations

Date: _____

Check in:

😊 🙂 😐 🙁

_____
_____
_____
_____
_____

Alignment Routine

Energy

Cleanse

Ground

Protect

Body

Movement

Breathwork

Stretch

Meditate

CHECK-UP

Ask the Tarot:
What energy should I
focus on or be aware of
today?

Ask the Tarot:
How can I embody
my highest good
today?

Reflection

Reflection

_____

_____

_____

_____

_____

_____

_____

_____

_____

_____

_____

_____

_____

_____

_____

_____

_____

_____

Questions to ponder

_____

_____

_____

_____

_____

_____

_____

_____

_____

 ## ACTIONABLE STEPS I CAN TAKE TO RELEASE/OVERCOME THIS BLOCK

THINGS I AM GRATEFUL FOR

1.

2.

3.

 Affirmations

Week 5

Date: _____

Check in:

_____

_____

_____

_____

_____

Alignment Routine

Energy

Cleanse

Ground

Protect

Meditate

Body

Movement

Breathwork

Stretch

DIAGNOSTIC TAROT SPREAD

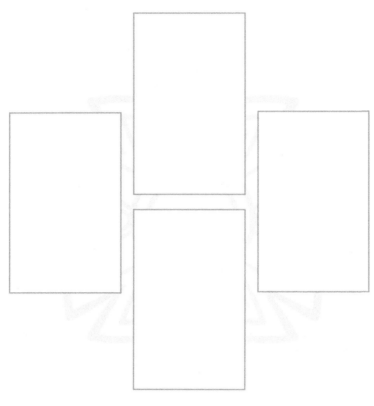

What block is the Tarot showing you?

_____

_____

_____

_____

_____

Reflection

Reflection

Reflection

_____

_____

_____

_____

_____

_____

_____

_____

_____

_____

_____

_____

_____

_____

_____

_____

_____

_____

_____

Questions to ponder

 ACTIONABLE STEPS I CAN TAKE TO RELEASE/OVERCOME THIS BLOCK

THINGS I AM GRATEFUL FOR

1.

2.

3.

Affirmations

_____

_____

_____

_____

_____

_____

_____

_____

Date: _____

Check in:

😊　🙂　😐　🙁

_____
_____
_____
_____
_____

Alignment Routine

Energy

Cleanse

Ground

Protect

Body

Movement

Breathwork

Stretch

Meditate

CHECK-UP

Ask the Tarot:
What energy should I
focus on or be aware of
today?

Ask the Tarot:
How can I embody
my highest good
today?

Reflection

Reflection

_____

_____

_____

_____

_____

_____

_____

_____

_____

_____

_____

_____

_____

_____

_____

_____

Questions to ponder

 ACTIONABLE STEPS I CAN TAKE TO RELEASE/OVERCOME THIS BLOCK

THINGS I AM GRATEFUL FOR

1.

2.

3.

Affirmations

_____

_____

_____

_____

_____

_____

_____

_____

Date: _____

Check in:

😊 🙂 😐 🙁

_____

_____

_____

_____

_____

Alignment Routine

Energy

Cleanse

Ground

Protect

Meditate

Body

Movement

Breathwork

Stretch

CHECK-UP

Ask the Tarot:
What energy should I
focus on or be aware of
today?

Ask the Tarot:
How can I embody
my highest good
today?

Reflection

Reflection

Questions to ponder

_____

_____

_____

_____

_____

_____

_____

_____

_____

 ## ACTIONABLE STEPS I CAN TAKE TO RELEASE/OVERCOME THIS BLOCK

THINGS I AM GRATEFUL FOR

1.

2.

3.

Affirmations

_____

_____

_____

_____

_____

_____

_____

_____

Date: _____

Check in:

_____
_____
_____
_____
_____

Alignment Routine

Energy

Cleanse

Ground

Protect

Meditate

Body

Movement

Breathwork

Stretch

CHECK-UP

Ask the Tarot:
What energy should I
focus on or be aware of
today?

Ask the Tarot:
How can I embody
my highest good
today?

Reflection

Reflection

Questions to ponder

_____

_____

_____

_____

_____

_____

_____

_____

_____

_____

 ACTIONABLE STEPS I CAN TAKE TO RELEASE/OVERCOME THIS BLOCK

THINGS I AM GRATEFUL FOR

1.

2.

3.

Affirmations

_____

_____

_____

_____

_____

_____

_____

_____

Date: _____

Check in:

😊 🙂 😐 🙁

_____
_____
_____
_____
_____

Alignment Routine

Energy

Cleanse

Ground

Protect

Body

Movement

Breathwork

Stretch

Meditate

CHECK-UP

Ask the Tarot:
What energy should I
focus on or be aware of
today?

Ask the Tarot:
How can I embody
my highest good
today?

Reflection

Reflection

Questions to ponder

_____

_____

_____

_____

_____

_____

_____

_____

_____

 ## ACTIONABLE STEPS I CAN TAKE TO RELEASE/OVERCOME THIS BLOCK

THINGS I AM GRATEFUL FOR

1.

2.

3.

Affirmations

_____

_____

_____

_____

_____

_____

_____

_____

Date: _____

Check in:

😊 🙂 😐 🙁

_____

_____

_____

_____

_____

Alignment Routine

Energy

Cleanse

Ground

Protect

Body

Movement

Breathwork

Stretch

Meditate

CHECK-UP

Ask the Tarot:
What energy should I
focus on or be aware of
today?

Ask the Tarot:
How can I embody
my highest good
today?

Reflection

Reflection

Questions to ponder

_____

_____

_____

_____

_____

_____

_____

_____

 ### ACTIONABLE STEPS I CAN TAKE TO RELEASE/OVERCOME THIS BLOCK

THINGS I AM GRATEFUL FOR

1.

2.

3.

Affirmations

Week 6

Date: _____

Check in:

😊 🙂 😐 🙁

_____
_____
_____
_____
_____

Alignment Routine

Energy

Cleanse

Ground

Protect

Body

Movement

Breathwork

Stretch

Meditate

DIAGNOSTIC TAROT SPREAD

What block is the Tarot showing you?

_____

_____

_____

_____

Reflection

Reflection

Reflection

Questions to ponder

_____

_____

_____

_____

_____

_____

_____

_____

_____

_____

 ACTIONABLE STEPS I CAN TAKE TO RELEASE/OVERCOME THIS BLOCK

THINGS I AM GRATEFUL FOR

1.

2.

3.

Affirmations

Date: _____

Check in:

_____
_____
_____
_____
_____

Alignment Routine

Energy

Cleanse

Ground

Protect

Meditate

Body

Movement

Breathwork

Stretch

CHECK-UP

Ask the Tarot:
What energy should I
focus on or be aware of
today?

Ask the Tarot:
How can I embody
my highest good
today?

Reflection

Reflection

Questions to ponder

 ACTIONABLE STEPS I CAN TAKE TO RELEASE/OVERCOME THIS BLOCK

THINGS I AM GRATEFUL FOR

1.

2.

3.

Affirmations

Date: _____

Check in:

😊 🙂 😐 🙁

_____
_____
_____
_____
_____

Alignment Routine

Energy

Cleanse

Ground

Protect

Body

Movement

Breathwork

Stretch

Meditate

CHECK-UP

Ask the Tarot:
What energy should I
focus on or be aware of
today?

Ask the Tarot:
How can I embody
my highest good
today?

Reflection

Reflection

Questions to ponder

_____

_____

_____

_____

_____

_____

_____

_____

_____

 ACTIONABLE STEPS I CAN TAKE TO RELEASE/OVERCOME THIS BLOCK

THINGS I AM GRATEFUL FOR

1.

2.

3.

Affirmations

_____

_____

_____

_____

_____

_____

_____

_____

_____

Date: _____

Check in:

🙂 🙂 😐 🙁

_____
_____
_____
_____
_____

Alignment Routine

Energy

Cleanse

Ground

Protect

Body

Movement

Breathwork

Stretch

Meditate

CHECK-UP

Ask the Tarot:
What energy should I
focus on or be aware of
today?

Ask the Tarot:
How can I embody
my highest good
today?

Reflection

_____

_____

_____

_____

_____

_____

_____

_____

_____

_____

_____

_____

_____

_____

_____

_____

_____

_____

_____

_____

Reflection

Questions to ponder

_____

_____

_____

_____

_____

_____

_____

_____

_____

 ACTIONABLE STEPS I CAN TAKE TO
RELEASE/OVERCOME THIS BLOCK

THINGS I AM GRATEFUL FOR

1.

2.

3.

Affirmations

_____

_____

_____

_____

_____

_____

_____

_____

Date: _____

Check in:

_____
_____
_____
_____
_____

Alignment Routine

Energy

Cleanse

Ground

Protect

Body

Movement

Breathwork

Stretch

Meditate

CHECK-UP

Ask the Tarot:
What energy should I
focus on or be aware of
today?

Ask the Tarot:
How can I embody
my highest good
today?

Reflection

_____

_____

_____

_____

_____

_____

_____

_____

_____

_____

_____

_____

_____

_____

_____

_____

_____

_____

_____

_____

_____

Reflection

Questions to ponder

_____

_____

_____

_____

_____

_____

_____

_____

 ACTIONABLE STEPS I CAN TAKE TO RELEASE/OVERCOME THIS BLOCK

THINGS I AM GRATEFUL FOR

1.

2.

3.

Affirmations

Date: _____

Check in:

😊 🙂 😐 🙁

✿

Alignment Routine

Energy

Cleanse

Ground

Protect

Body

Movement

Breathwork

Stretch

Meditate

CHECK-UP

Ask the Tarot:
What energy should I
focus on or be aware of
today?

Ask the Tarot:
How can I embody
my highest good
today?

Reflection

_____

_____

_____

_____

_____

_____

_____

_____

_____

_____

_____

_____

_____

_____

_____

_____

_____

_____

_____

_____

_____

Reflection

Questions to ponder

_____

_____

_____

_____

_____

_____

_____

_____

_____

 ACTIONABLE STEPS I CAN TAKE TO RELEASE/OVERCOME THIS BLOCK

THINGS I AM GRATEFUL FOR

1.

2.

3.

Affirmations

Week 7

Date: _____

Check in:

☺ ☺ 😐 ☹

_____

_____

_____

_____

_____

Alignment Routine

Energy

Cleanse

Ground

Protect

Body

Movement

Breathwork

Stretch

Meditate

DIAGNOSTIC TAROT SPREAD

What block is the Tarot showing you?

Reflection

Reflection

Reflection

Questions to ponder

 ACTIONABLE STEPS I CAN TAKE TO RELEASE/OVERCOME THIS BLOCK

THINGS I AM GRATEFUL FOR

1.

2.

3.

 Affirmations

Date: _____

Check in:

_____
_____
_____
_____
_____

Alignment Routine

Energy

Cleanse

Ground

Protect

Body

Movement

Breathwork

Stretch

Meditate

CHECK-UP

Ask the Tarot:
What energy should I
focus on or be aware of
today?

Ask the Tarot:
How can I embody
my highest good
today?

Reflection

Reflection

Questions to ponder

_____

_____

_____

_____

_____

_____

_____

_____

_____

 ## ACTIONABLE STEPS I CAN TAKE TO RELEASE/OVERCOME THIS BLOCK

THINGS I AM GRATEFUL FOR

1.

2.

3.

Affirmations

Date: _____

Check in:

_____
_____
_____
_____
_____

Alignment Routine

Energy

Cleanse

Ground

Protect

Body

Movement

Breathwork

Stretch

Meditate

CHECK-UP

Ask the Tarot:
What energy should I
focus on or be aware of
today?

Ask the Tarot:
How can I embody
my highest good
today?

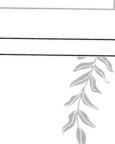

Reflection

Reflection

Questions to ponder

_____
_____
_____
_____
_____
_____
_____
_____
_____

 ACTIONABLE STEPS I CAN TAKE TO RELEASE/OVERCOME THIS BLOCK

THINGS I AM GRATEFUL FOR

1.

2.

3.

Affirmations

_____

_____

_____

_____

_____

_____

_____

_____

Date: _____

Check in:

😊 🙂 😐 🙁

_____
_____
_____
_____
_____

Alignment Routine

Energy

Cleanse

Ground

Protect

Body

Movement

Breathwork

Stretch

Meditate

CHECK-UP

Ask the Tarot:
What energy should I
focus on or be aware of
today?

Ask the Tarot:
How can I embody
my highest good
today?

Reflection

_____
_____
_____
_____
_____
_____
_____
_____
_____
_____
_____
_____
_____
_____
_____
_____
_____
_____
_____
_____
_____

Reflection

Questions to ponder

_____

_____

_____

_____

_____

_____

_____

_____

_____

 ## ACTIONABLE STEPS I CAN TAKE TO
RELEASE/OVERCOME THIS BLOCK

THINGS I AM GRATEFUL FOR

1.

2.

3.

Affirmations

Date: _____

Check in:

😊 🙂 😐 🙁

_____

_____

_____

_____

_____

Alignment Routine

Energy

Cleanse

Ground

Protect

Body

Movement

Breathwork

Stretch

Meditate

CHECK-UP

Ask the Tarot:
What energy should I
focus on or be aware of
today?

Ask the Tarot:
How can I embody
my highest good
today?

Reflection

Reflection

Questions to ponder

_____

_____

_____

_____

_____

_____

_____

_____

 ## ACTIONABLE STEPS I CAN TAKE TO RELEASE/OVERCOME THIS BLOCK

THINGS I AM GRATEFUL FOR

1.

2.

3.

Affirmations

_____

_____

_____

_____

_____

_____

_____

_____

Date: _____

Check in:

😊 🙂 😐 ☹️

_____
_____
_____
_____
_____

Alignment Routine

Energy

Cleanse

Ground

Protect

Body

Movement

Breathwork

Stretch

Meditate

CHECK-UP

Ask the Tarot:
What energy should I
focus on or be aware of
today?

Ask the Tarot:
How can I embody
my highest good
today?

Reflection

_____

_____

_____

_____

_____

_____

_____

_____

_____

_____

_____

_____

_____

_____

_____

_____

_____

_____

_____

_____

Reflection

Questions to ponder

_____

_____

_____

_____

_____

_____

_____

_____

_____

 ACTIONABLE STEPS I CAN TAKE TO RELEASE/OVERCOME THIS BLOCK

THINGS I AM GRATEFUL FOR

1.

2.

3.

Affirmations

_____
_____
_____
_____
_____
_____
_____
_____
_____

Week 8

Date: _____

Check in:

😊 🙂 😐 🙁

_____
_____
_____
_____
_____

Alignment Routine

Energy

Cleanse

Ground

Protect

Body

Movement

Breathwork

Stretch

Meditate

DIAGNOSTIC TAROT SPREAD

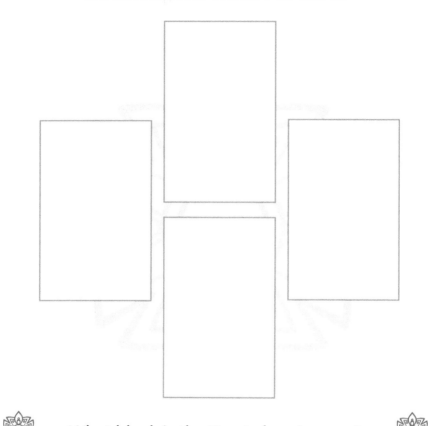

What block is the Tarot showing you?

_____

_____

_____

_____

_____

Reflection

Reflection

Reflection

Questions to ponder

 ACTIONABLE STEPS I CAN TAKE TO RELEASE/OVERCOME THIS BLOCK

THINGS I AM GRATEFUL FOR

1.

2.

3.

Affirmations

_____

_____

_____

_____

_____

_____

_____

_____

Date: _____

Check in:

😊 🙂 😐 🙁

_____
_____
_____
_____
_____

Alignment Routine

Energy

Cleanse

Ground

Protect

Body

Movement

Breathwork

Stretch

Meditate

CHECK-UP

Ask the Tarot:
What energy should I
focus on or be aware of
today?

Ask the Tarot:
How can I embody
my highest good
today?

Reflection

Reflection

Questions to ponder

 **ACTIONABLE STEPS I CAN TAKE TO
RELEASE/OVERCOME THIS BLOCK**

THINGS I AM GRATEFUL FOR

1.

2.

3.

Affirmations

_____

_____

_____

_____

_____

_____

_____

_____

_____

Date: _____

Check in:

😊 🙂 😐 🙁

_____
_____
_____
_____
_____

Alignment Routine

Energy

Cleanse

Ground

Protect

Body

Movement

Breathwork

Stretch

Meditate

CHECK-UP

Ask the Tarot:
What energy should I
focus on or be aware of
today?

Ask the Tarot:
How can I embody
my highest good
today?

Reflection

Reflection

Questions to ponder

_____
_____
_____
_____
_____
_____
_____
_____
_____

 ## ACTIONABLE STEPS I CAN TAKE TO RELEASE/OVERCOME THIS BLOCK

THINGS I AM GRATEFUL FOR

1.

2.

3.

 Affirmations

Date: _____

Check in:

😊 🙂 😐 🙁

_____

_____

_____

_____

_____

Alignment Routine

Energy

Cleanse

Ground

Protect

Body

Movement

Breathwork

Stretch

Meditate

CHECK-UP

Ask the Tarot:
What energy should I
focus on or be aware of
today?

Ask the Tarot:
How can I embody
my highest good
today?

Reflection

Reflection

Questions to ponder

_____

_____

_____

_____

_____

_____

_____

_____

 ACTIONABLE STEPS I CAN TAKE TO
RELEASE/OVERCOME THIS BLOCK

THINGS I AM GRATEFUL FOR

1.

2.

3.

Affirmations

_____

_____

_____

_____

_____

_____

_____

_____

_____

Date: _____

Check in:

_____
_____
_____
_____
_____

Alignment Routine

Energy

Cleanse

Ground

Protect

Body

Movement

Breathwork

Stretch

Meditate

CHECK-UP

Ask the Tarot:
What energy should I
focus on or be aware of
today?

Ask the Tarot:
How can I embody
my highest good
today?

Reflection

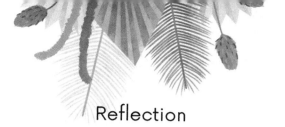

Reflection

Questions to ponder

_____

_____

_____

_____

_____

_____

_____

_____

_____

 ## ACTIONABLE STEPS I CAN TAKE TO RELEASE/OVERCOME THIS BLOCK

THINGS I AM GRATEFUL FOR

1.

2.

3.

Affirmations

_____

_____

_____

_____

_____

_____

_____

_____

_____

Date: _____

Check in:

😊 🙂 😐 ☹️

_____
_____
_____
_____
_____

Alignment Routine

Energy

Cleanse

Ground

Protect

Meditate

Body

Movement

Breathwork

Stretch

CHECK-UP

Ask the Tarot:
What energy should I
focus on or be aware of
today?

Ask the Tarot:
How can I embody
my highest good
today?

Reflection

_____
_____
_____
_____
_____
_____
_____
_____
_____
_____
_____
_____
_____
_____
_____
_____
_____
_____
_____
_____

Reflection

Questions to ponder

 ACTIONABLE STEPS I CAN TAKE TO RELEASE/OVERCOME THIS BLOCK

THINGS I AM GRATEFUL FOR

1.

2.

3.

Affirmations

Made in the USA
Columbia, SC
27 November 2022

71860697R00189